A Coach's Handbook

Maximizing the Hitting and Pitching Skills of a Younger Baseball Player

Thoughts by Jeff Gutjahr

ISBN: 1-4140-2779-6 (e-book)
ISBN: 1-4140-2778-8 (Paperback)

This book is printed on acid free paper.

1stBooks - rev. 12/15/03

To my parents, for their endless love and support with all of the activities I found interest in growing up. Especially to Dad when it came to baseball. Thanks for always finding time to have a "catch"

To my students and players, for helping me grow as a teacher and coach. Your respect and confidence in me has been everything a young teacher in the early stages of his career could ask for. You have all inspired me in your own unique way.

Table of contents

Pregame

When I first sat down to do this, it was never my intent to set out and write a book. My purpose was to reflect upon the achievements of the past season and document what worked and what didn't. I've only been coaching high school baseball for 5 years, at this point, so my biggest objective was simply to organize my pile of coaching notes on post-it's, napkins, palm-pilots, etc. Somewhere along the line, though, this "handbook" for coaching evolved.

In doing this, it is not my intention to claim that I know all there is to know about coaching the game of baseball. In fact, I am comfortable in admitting I still have a lot to learn. I am comfortable because anyone who chooses a career in education and in coaching had better be open to the thoughts and suggestions of others. After all, if I were going to teach one of my players or students something new, it would be beneficial to first have their respect. Constantly, as a teacher and coach, I am trying to find a way to relate to my students. In doing so, somewhere along the line I hope to gain that respect. When I show that I, too, am interested in improving my knowledge of a given subject, they realize that I truly care about their progress as well. From this, they buy into what I am saying and they work harder.

Every good educator understands that finding success in the classroom cannot be done without some help. My hope in organizing my thoughts on paper was to help my colleagues at the levels below mine understand better what it is I look for when their players arrive at my level. Similar to my classroom experience, I know our Calculus teachers and our PreCalculus teachers, or Algebra 1 and Algebra 2 teachers are constantly comparing notes to ensure each student is prepared when they enroll in their next math course. From this experience, everyone works together to provide a consistent, productive learning environment. This, too, I hope is a true pattern that any successful high school baseball program follows between their Freshman, Junior Varsity, and Varsity levels. Ideally, it would be great for the middle school coaches to be consistent as well with what is being done at the high school.

<u>A Coach's Handbook</u> is a contribution to the varying philosophies on the game of baseball. Its focus is on, to me, the two most important aspects of the game, pitching and hitting. It is simply meant to be a collection of suggestions to use in coaching young athletes.

The game of baseball is a wonderful game. The more experience one has had at playing it, the more that person has to offer as a coach. It bothers me to see at the high school level that there are often times coaches who have had little experience with the game given the right to work with and influence young minds. For some, coaching is simply a way to earn a little extra pay on top of their teacher's salary. Their teams have sloppy, undisciplined approaches and often there is noticeable talent going to waste because of the lack of proper guidance. Sure, this is a simple game, but its finer points for the inexperienced can expose a coach's ignorance.

As coaches, we may not always have the most gifted baseball players to deal with. However, it is what you get out of the ones you have that will make the difference. In my young career, I am confident that I have been able to find a way to relate to my players at some level. Whether the wins have come or not, I know that those who wanted to improve their games did, and those who didn't have great aspirations of a future in baseball were able to take something from the experience as well.

The notes and illustrations I have compiled to create this book are based on approaches to the game of baseball that I believe in strongly and build my program around. I would be arrogant to say that these are all my own original ideas. They are not. However, they are my perception of what goes into making a sound fundamental hitter and pitcher.

Jeff Gutjahr

I hope in some way this book helps to inspire you in your coaching. I hope, too, that you, like I, will continue to observe the philosophies of others on the game so we can each continue to build and understand our own beliefs concerning the game. Either way, good luck in your coaching adventures, and for those days when the energy seems distant, may the inspiration of knowing you are truly making a difference in the lives of young people carry you through.

Hitting

If not to educate, then to refresh...that is my philosophy. There is so much we learn from our time on the diamond, that sometimes we do not spend enough time reflecting on what we know. My goal with this section is to break down the finer parts of the swing and give you my take on how to present it to kids. By breaking things down, I'm hoping to give you a better understanding of what to look for when a kid first comes to you to swing a bat, and a better idea of how to handle many common faults that can occur. My approach is not meant to be rocket science, but simply an accumulation of thoughts and ideas, both my own and of others, that I have found to work for myself. These notes are notes that I have made over the last several years of coaching, and I would encourage you in your own coaching to make similar notes of things you hear or do that you find do or do not work in your approach. Every once in a while, I find it beneficial to go back to the notes I've made to refresh and organize my own beliefs. For me, being able to write things out in an organized manner (much like my approach here) is a great way to know just how well I come across to my players in explaining to them the art of hitting.

***

My philosophy on hitting is to keep things as simple as possible. If I notice a kid having a problem with their swing, then the best way to fix that problem and see immediate feedback is to give them some soft toss or work from a tee. I don't try to get to technical. If there is a drill I can implement, then I have them try it. If there are several faults to their swing, then I just try to take what I see is the biggest fault, and give them a swing thought or two to focus on for that particular day, or, depending on how big the fault is, that week. Basically, these are the steps I look for:

Stance

A foundation for a solid swing is built off of an athletic stance at the plate. In fact, I like to think of the swing in two parts: There's the base, where we discuss the stance and step; then there's the upper body that is involved in the swing.

I think a good visual to keep in mind as a hitter steps in to swing is as they take their set up to the plate their base should be engaged just as it is when they are playing defense. All good fielders have a set up in the field where they have bend in their knees and waist as well as their weight evenly distributed on the balls of their feet. Having the weight on the balls of their feet is so important for a couple of reasons. First, it helps players as they step to avoid having their front foot open too much. Usually, if the weight is in the heals, the stride will be open. Second, the pivot of the back foot can only occur if the weight is focused in the proper part of the foot. It is set to "squish the bug" so to speak.

Usually to help a player understand the idea of a solid base, I will have them set up to plate and then give them a little nudge square in their chest. If they fall backwards then their weight is too much in their heels. The width of the player's stance also is an important idea in this weight distribution aspect. I feel that a player should have a width to their stance where their feet are about half way between shoulder width and double shoulder width. If they are at shoulder width with their stance, I feel that the player is too tall and their base isn't engaged to hit the ball. In other words, I don't feel like the player is really ready to hit. If their feet are too far apart, then there is concern for the player having poor weight distribution when they execute the swing. What I usually see here, is a player having difficulty keeping their weight transfer through the ball centered transferring forward slightly.

In taking their stance to the plate, players should set up to the plate so that their front foot is in line with a line that can be extended through the top corners of the plate. Their distance from the plate should be such that they can comfortably bend at their waste and reach out with their bottom hand on the bat being able to touch the far opposite corner of the plate with the top of the bat.

Stance at the plate

Setting up to the plate giving the hitter complete plate coverage

Step

Now that we're set up to the plate let's advance to the role that the base plays as the pitch is delivered. As the ball gets to the point where it will leave the pitcher's hand, the player should have a weight distribution between their front and back side that is close to 50-50. As the ball is leaving the pitcher's hand, the player steps but his weight distribution is still 50-50. Any weight distribution forward, I feel, forces the hitter too much to his front side leaving him vulnerable to the outside pitch.

A quiet step, but base is still engaged

If the player has a compact approach in mind, his step should be "quiet". By quiet, I am looking for a stride that is no further than the line, which could be extended off of the front edge of the plate. Remembering that the player's weight is focused on the balls of his feet, if the player is stepping quietly, he will avoid stepping open.

At this point there are a couple of things I would like to clarify. I've stressed the importance of players having a stride that allows them to step "closed" with the front foot. Obviously, you have to be cognizant of the player's physical make up. For whatever reason, whether it's flexibility, double jointed, or whatever, some player's will only be able to step closed to a point. The importance of this idea is that the mindset is to step closed. If they have that focus in mind and they are stepping to the balls of their feet, then their practicing the right technique.

While we're on the idea of a player's physical make up, it is also worth mentioning that some player's may choose to stand more upright or wider than what I am suggesting. Every player is different, and in teaching hitting, it should be done so on an individual basis. Lecturing to an entire group of players on hitting is not that beneficial. If you as a coach, have given the chance to your players to swing the bat and have gotten around to all of them to talk about one or two things you like or dislike about their swing, then addressing them as a group has more merit. You can then stand in front of the group and address common problems that you may be seeing and how you would suggest to fix them. Certain players will have a tremendous amount of natural ability, and if they do certain things that may not be a part of your philosophy or the ones I am suggesting, but they show that they hit the ball well, then you may want to leave well enough alone. Worry more with them about their approach when it comes to hitting live. Nothing irritates me more as a coach to see a naturally gifted kid, a good kid, who wants to be the best ball player they can be, get all screwed up by some coach or instructor who makes changes to his swing that weren't a problem in the first place, just so he can hit that coach or instructor's "way".

Getting back on track now, finally, I want to clarify what I mean by "squishing the bug". As the player comes to a finish in his swing, where his weight is centered to slightly ahead of center, his back foot should pivot. The more ahead of center the player is with his weight distribution the more his back foot will be to being on his toe. Either way, if a player has the mind set that their weight should be on the balls of their feet to begin with, to get a feel for a proper pivot, the player can visualize squishing a bug with their back foot. If he really wants to squish the bug thoroughly, the heel will be off the ground somewhat significantly as the foot pivots back and forth on the ball of the foot. Some coaches don't like this idea, because they feel that this concept institutes a picture in the player's mind that their weight will fall backwards forcing the player to loose their foundation as well as their upper half, which will result in lofting the ball in the air. While I understand that argument, that visual is only accurate if the hitters back foot is close to flat. If that happens, then the player doesn't have the right approach anyway. If their focus is on having the weight in the ball of the foot, that won't happen.

Two hand follow through (note the pivot and weight
distribution)

One hand follow through (notice how in either follow
through the hands finish at head level behind the
hitter)

Grip

The grip of the swing to me, is like the hinges on a door. When you take a door off its hinges and then try to put it back on, if you don't get the pieces inserted correctly, the door is not going to open and close very smoothly. The same can be said about the hands placed on a bat.

I think the most popular school of thought I've ever heard on how a bat should lie in your hands is to make sure when you place your hands on a bat, your knuckles are aligned. Although, I don't feel they have to be perfectly aligned, it is a good thought.

By having the mindset that your knuckles need to be aligned it forces you to get the bat up towards the top of your palm so the majority of your bat is being controlled in your fingers. It's a nice loose feeling that allows for you to swing with better bat speed. It's like the difference between a pitchers fastball grip and his change up grip. If a pitcher is looking to take something off the ball, he is going to place more fingers on the ball, and set the ball further back in his hand. This creates slower velocity. If a hitter holds his bat back in his hands so that it is basically resting at the base of his thumb, he is limiting the bat's potential to create speed. It is restricted by the amount of hand on the handle.

A good procedure to run through to ensure a proper grip is to lay your bat on the floor and pick it up so that you hands are aligned with your fingers on top of one another where they can easily wrap around the bat in picking it up.

Essentially, you're picking the bat up with your fingers, so they will encompass the majority of the bat's handle. After you've picked up the bat, bring it to rest on your shoulder so that the bat is pointing directly behind you. From here, if you lift the bat slightly from your shoulder, you're hands are in a perfect position to begin the actual swing.

Your arms are also in a good position, because the elbows are not a noticeable factor. The old idea of the back elbow having to be up so that a hitter can be ready to swing is taken out of play. The hands are what need to be up (shoulder or slightly above), not the back elbow.

Hands

So far, we've discussed three aspects of the swing without even swinging the bat. Well, if you're not set up correctly in the first place, the actual execution of the swing will not produce the results we're looking for anyway. In other words, you can't build the house, without laying down the foundation first.

Even though, the stance, step, and grip are essential to being able to swing the bat, the hands ultimately are the key to its overall execution (assuming everything previous is sound). I've mentioned that as the pitch is beginning to leave the pitcher's hand, the player takes his step. At the same time, many coaches believe the hands should "trigger". What that means is the hands will move slightly back from their original position. I don't believe this is an overly important aspect of the execution of the swing. I feel it is more of a natural thing that certain hitters do. I don't like to stress the trigger, because I just feel like it is one more thing for the hitter to think about. If they do it with their step, great. If not, that's fine, too. The important thing is that if a player does move his hands, make sure the hands don't drop from their original position or rise too much. Either direction, will require more rerouting in the hands to get the bat in the proper position to swing and there simply is not enough time as a pitch is delivered to make excessive, unnecessary adjustments.

As the pitch is on it's way, the mind commits to the idea that it is going to swing until the last possible split second. At that last possible second the hands start the swing of the bat. Understand, as the hands start the swing, everything else will follow naturally. Things like the hitter's front side opening or hips clearing or what have you, will happen as a result of the hand movement. The idea of the hands moving before everything else does is a pretty significant idea, especially when we address the idea of hitting something off speed versus sitting on a fastball. You often hear the expression "weight back" to adjust to hitting an off speed pitch and avoid being too far out in front. I actually find that expression misleading. If I'm looking for an even weight distribution between the front and back side as I'm looking at a hitter, the last thing I want him to do is start to lean further back in his swing to keep his "weight back". This is why I think it is important to implement in a hitter's mind the idea that the *hands* should stay back until they're absolutely ready to hit the pitch.

The hands start by taking the bat down a "slide". The hands travel so that they move to a point where the hands have gone down the slide while the barrel of the bat is level with the back shoulder (close to where the hands began originally—let me reemphasize again, with the pictures I've included, I can better illustrate what I mean in words. I would never be this technical in presenting the swing to my players. This is simply some checkpoints that I would look for in my players swing. If I happen to see that players are not getting into the proper positions then I will pull them aside and show them what they are doing versus what it should look like. Only then, will I worry about being technical, simply to help them understand what they are doing wrong and why they need to adjust).

Bat in "slide" position

As the hands get to the bottom of the slide, so far the bottom hand has been the integral factor. The power of the swing is still being stored ready to be unleashed. Now, the top hand takes over. The top hand fires the barrel of the bat through the zone so that at full extension, the hitter is pointing the bat out at a 45-degree angle to the line drawn off the front edge of the plate extended.

From this point of extension, the majority of the power of the swing is being released. However, to completely exhaust all of the energy stored in the swing, the top hand continues firing the bat through the zone to a point where the hands are finishing near head level. To me, both hands finishing on the bat is not the important part of the finish of the swing. The important part is noticing where the top hand finishes. If the top hand is doing its job, it will finish near head level behind the batter's head (see previous pictures). When the top hand is not firing through, I notice that a hitter who likes to let go with one hand of the bat will have his top hand finish somewhere in front of him. If the hitter is doing this, then ideally he is primarily swinging with his bottom hand and is losing most of the power of the swing. If you use wiffle balls or tennis balls for soft toss, you have to be careful in looking out for this. This is common in soft toss because of the force it requires to hit the ball into the net. A bad habit like this can carry over to a game situation. At contact the hitter's bat will look like it recoils, driving the barrel with greater force backwards rather than forwards.

Focus

In fine-tuning the swing on the tee or with soft toss, every swing should be executed with the intent to produce a line drive up the middle or the other way. If tossing, the tosses should be thrown from about a forty-five degree angle in front of the batter with the ball being met by the bat somewhere between the belt and the knees...no higher or lower. If the ball is to be hit up the middle or the other way, the hitter should be meeting the ball at the plate or slightly back of the front of the plate.

In practicing a fundamental soft toss routine, the hitter will focus on hitting the ball as it reaches the green position pictured above. From this position the hitter will be able to drive the ball the other way with success.

This is important. Players hitting balls that are tossed in front of the plate are only working on inside pitches. When a hitter steps in the box during a game or during batting practice, their objective every time they see a pitch is to drive it back at the pitcher or over the head of the appropriate opposite middle infielder's head. If this is their focus, then, when a pitch is thrown inside, their hands will recognize they have a pitch they can pull hard, thus speeding up the hands to meet the ball in front of the plate where an inside pitch is hit. This adjustment can be easily made if they have the proper focus. If you reverse this focus, in other words, the hitter approaches with the intent to pull everything, adjusting to an outside pitch is impossible.

Hitting does not have to be complicated. If you have the idea you are going to try to drive the ball up the middle or the other way every time, all of the repetition of soft toss and tee work will take over when a hitter takes his place in the box. However, there is one thing that is important to make clear at this point. If we understand the science of hitting, an inside pitch is met in front of the plate with the bat, a pitch down the middle is met just as the ball is approaching the plate, and an outside pitch should be met as the ball is over the back half of the plate. Three different pitches does not mean three different swings. The hands will make the adjustment to where contact with the ball will be made. The hands will speed up on the inside pitch. The hands will stay back a bit longer to meet the outside pitch. Otherwise, the swing is the same once the hands go. Hitting would be impossible, if there had to be three different swings for three different pitches. There is simply not enough time to process what the pitch is out of the pitchers hand, which corner of the plate it is going to go over, and which swing to use given the pitch. A hitter has a split second to make a decision on a pitch. They have to be confident that no matter what they're decision is to do with the pitch, that all of the rehearsal of practice will simply take over in firing the hands to execute their one swing.

Meeting the inside pitch

Meeting the pitch down the middle

Meeting the outside pitch

Before moving on, a couple of other thoughts to consider in teaching a hitter good focus at the plate. One, is what to do with a curveball? How can you teach a kid to hit a curveball? While there are drills that can be implemented to simulate off speed pitches, ultimately, the best way for a hitter to learn how to hit a curve ball is to see it through playing. The more a person plays the game of baseball, the better they will get at recognizing a curveball out of the pitchers hand and knowing how to handle it. To me, the best thing to tell a kid about how to hit a curveball is to not bother with it. Unless, a hitter has two strikes on him, he should be looking for something he can handle. For all good hitters, they will be sitting on a fastball to drive. This now leads into my other thought as far as how to approach hitting in the box.

When a hitter first steps in the box, he should look to hit the first pitch only if it is in his "zone". By this, I mean the hitter should look for the ball in a spot that he likes to see the ball. It's a spot, where through practice, he has figured out that he can cut loose and drive the pitch. A hitter should look for a ball in his spot and then commit to hitting any pitch within about 6 inches left or right, high or low, of that spot. If it's not there, whether it is a strike or not, don't worry about hitting the pitch until you, the hitter, have fallen behind in the count. When a hitter gets one strike on him during an at bat with a count more in the pitcher's favor, that length of 6 inches has to expand to somewhere between 9-12 inches. At two strikes, the hitter's spot they are looking for, becomes the entire strike zone. Good hitters know what their strikes are, and understand that just because the pitch is a strike, depending on the count, it is not a pitch they absolutely have to hit.

Helpful Drills

When it comes to ways to emphasize a solid, fundamentally sound swing, some coaches may find it beneficial to include drills in with their everyday soft toss and tee work regimens. While I think that is a good idea, I personally feel that takes away from the time that I want to spend working on other aspects of the game.

There are some things that individual kids do well already as hitters. I like to give my kids a regimen of soft toss or tee work reps to work on before stepping in the cage or on the field for BP. While this workout doesn't contain specific drills I have detailed in the proceeding, as I go around to each station and assess my players approach, I may pull them aside after a set and discuss with them what I see in their swing. I try to be positive about what they are doing well and then constructive about what they need to work on getting better at. Often, one of these drills is nice to implement with different individual players, just so they have a better understanding of the position they need to try and get themselves into to maximize their potential to hit the ball well. These drills are good to develop that visual and feel to give the player instant feedback. If you work with them as a coach on hitting when they are working at soft toss or on a tee, they can easily see the benefits of what you are telling them. It's a quick, simple practice method where in controlling the toss of the ball or the level of the ball on the tee, the way the ball jumps off the bat can be easily seen and felt by the player.

Here are some drills to consider:

- *No step soft toss or tee work.* For myself, this is something I like to implement in my regular soft toss regimen starting on the first day of practice. I discuss with the players the importance of a comfortable, athletic stance where their base is engaged and the weight is in the balls of their feet (as I have discussed earlier). With this being stressed, the players take their reps with no step. Everything else that occurs during the swing will still take place, whether it takes place in the upper or lower body. The only difference is the front foot won't move forward. I find this is beneficial to quiet down the swing and take away the possibility of the player stepping "in the bucket". In other words, the player is striding with his foot open or stepping so that his entire stance is open. The player is forced to stay closed with the hips by taking out the step. Naturally, as the swing is made, the front side will clear and the hips will open more. This is simply a technique to force the player into the correct position to unload the hands on the ball. Their foundation is still in tact. I find after about a week of practicing this drill, when I let the players put the step back in, those who have truly worked at the drill, take a step that is minimal. If they had been someone who stepped "in the bucket", this dilemma has been significantly improved for the better.

- *Better Extension:* Often when I walk around to soft toss stations during practice, I notice kids who have hands that break down too quickly. By this, I mean they are letting they're hands roll over sooner then would be ideal to hit a baseball with authority. To correct this, I have the player take their bat and line himself up to a wall (a net would be preferable) so that the distance between him and the wall is the length of the bat.

From here, the player takes his stance and the first couple of times for feel, slowly the player drives his hands down the "slide" I've mentioned earlier. At the bottom of the slide, the top hand fires the bat over (remember at first, take it slow), and if the hands are getting the proper extension, the bat should be able to swing through without hitting the wall. Besides the player hitting the wall, one thing that needs to be observed is the hitter's upper body. Sometimes a hitter, to avoid hitting the wall, will pull away with his upper half. This would prove counterproductive to the player's overall swing. This is why using a net, like the side of the batting cage or an L-screen, might be the best option.

Driving the hands forward for better extension so that the bat will clear the fence during the execution of the swing.

How the execution of wall drill should look as swing follows through

Avoid pulling away from the wall with the upper half

- *Weak Top Hand*: The main reason a player does not hit the ball on a line or struggles with hitting the other way with authority is due to the aggressiveness of the hands. While both hands are necessary to hit the ball with authority, the top hand might be the most vital. When I am assessing my hitters approach taking tosses on the side, if I notice they are dropping the barrel of the bat through the zone and the ball of the bat is coming off with a fly ball trajectory, their top hand is not aggressive enough.

Also, sometimes a hitter may finish where his hands are breaking after contact, but as their bottom hand continues with the follow through, the top hand stops and finishes in front of the player rather then high and behind his head as mentioned previously. Using the extension drill mentioned previously, if a player can get that feel where he has driven his hands to the bottom of the slide, from there, it is simply a matter of firing the top hand over. During soft toss and tee work, a hitter could take his stance to the ball and move to the position where the hands have been driven to the point where the top hand should take over (the bottom of the slide). From this position, he can take his tosses or hit from the tee, where his only focus is to fire the top hand over. This is great to stress the importance of firing the top hand over as well as beneficial to building strength in the forearms.

A hitter, could also take soft toss from his knees, where he chokes up near the top of the handle of the bat with only his top hand holding the bat (using a lighter bat like a fungo might be better). His bottom hand is placed under his right arm (right handed hitter), so that the only part of the body that will be involved in the execution of the swing, is the top hand and right arm.

Because the hitter has choked up on the bat, he will be forced to key in on the idea of an aggressive top hand that fires through. If he does not have the correct approach the bottom of the bat will knick the hitter in the forearm. It will be added incentive to do it correctly to avoid it being painful and bruising up the forearm.

- *Weight Distribution*: When a hitter takes his swing, he comes to a finish that is under control where the weight is still centered or slightly ahead of center. Sometimes a hitter will struggle with his weight finishing too much on his backside.

You can see this problem in the way the heel of back foot stays too close to the ground as it pivots and/or the upper half of the body is significantly tilted towards the backside.

On the other hand, a hitter may also struggle with his weight finishing or transferring too quickly to the front side leaving him vulnerable to pitches on the outer part of the plate.

To correct the problem of the weight falling back too far at or after contact, I would suggest giving the hitter a fungo and have him either toss to himself and try to hit line drives into a net that are about belt high or simply be incorporated into practice as an additional fungo hitter for the infielders. You'll notice when a team takes pregame how the coach (if he's any good) hits ground balls to the infielders or even fly balls to the outfielders finishing with his weight on his front leg. This is comparable to where a golfer would finish his swing or even a tennis player. This is a good drill for a player to develop that sensation of keeping his weight more forward than what he is use to. In gaining that feel, when he goes to take soft toss, from his proper hitting stance, he'll have a better feel and understanding for when he finishes with too much weight on his backside. As far as someone who is too much on their front side at contact. To correct this, I want to first go back to my fungo example. You might ask yourself, if you want a player to hit a baseball with good weight distribution, then why don't you approach everything like you're hitting a fungo? While I like how the fungo keeps the weight honest, I don't like how the base is working. In hitting a fungo, you are more upright and tall in your stance. The legs are not bent as much, which to me, doesn't give me the feel that I'm really ready to hit when I'm in the box. My suggestion for a player who is more of a "front foot" hitter is to widen their stance a bit (as I described in the earlier section entitled "stance"). If they're not doing so already, bend more at the knees. With a wider stance, it will be harder for the hitter to sway their weight significantly back or forth, making it hard to be too far forward in their swing.

- *Off speed problems:* Not being able to hit an off speed pitch, whether it is a curveball or change up, is a result of two things. One, is recognition. The only way a player will get better at hitting off speed pitches (which should only be their concern with two strikes) is to see those pitches thrown at them. Therefore, game situations are important, whether the hitter is in the box or picking up things from the bench. Only so much can be simulated in B.P. Second, once the pitch is recognized, the hands need to take over. The hands must stay back where they've positioned themselves after the step, until the pitch has reached the plate, then unload to swing the bat.

A great way to practice this is to take soft toss where the feeder tosses a sequence of flatter tosses to the hitter (simulating fastballs) and then mixes in a more lofted toss.

The toss gets no higher than the hitter's shoulders, and the idea is for the ball to land and be hit in the same spot in the zone as the fastball tosses. If a player is meeting the ball in front of the plate or hitting it before it has reached a level that is between the hitter's belt and knees, then the hands are not staying back long enough. When a hitter can perform this drill where they can go back and forth between hitting the fastball simulated toss and the off speed toss they have disciplined themselves to be a good two strike hitter. Before he can do this, though, he should probably just practice tossing with sets that involve all off speed pitches to get the proper feel.

- *Tracking (Head on the Ball)*: "Keep your eye on the ball..."—an important set of directions in teaching hitting. If a hitter is not keeping his eyes on the ball, then he is not keeping his head on the ball. If the head is not staying on the ball, then the shoulders are not staying closed, which can cause the hips to rotate to early, which can...well, I think you see my point. It's one big chain reaction. It should be fundamental practice for a hitter to see every pitch either to contact with his bat, or, if he is taking the pitch, through to the catcher's mitt. Early in the preseason when it is hard to get outside for practice and simulate live throwing, I like to have hitters stand in for my pitchers as they get in their work. By doing this, we're accomplishing a couple of things. One, the hitter gets to at least see a pitcher throw live to them. He can focus on keeping a quiet base as he steps and quiet hands as he keeps the hands back (while they trigger...no swing, of course). Second, the hitter can practice seeing the ball all the way through to the catcher's mitt. He can really exaggerate this idea, so that in game situations it will be engrained in his approach, thus easier to execute in a game situation.

Another drill I like to incorporate from time to time as I see a player struggling with staying on the ball is a reverse toss-type drill. Usually, I like players to toss to each other from about a 45-degree angle in front of the hitter. I have the tosser take this same approach, only instead of being in front of the hitter, the tosser takes his position from the back. The hitter still simulates the ball coming from the front by looking forward with his head in taking his stance. As the tosser is ready to feed the ball to the hitter, he prompts the hitter with the word "ball". When the hitter hears this prompt, he steps (and triggers) and turns his head back to pick up the ball. With the same focus as normal soft toss he tries to hit the ball up the middle or the other way. It is important for the feeder in this drill, also, to make sure his tosses are landing in the proper zones to hit.

This is a tough drill to execute. As a coach, you have to be careful to look out for kids dropping their shoulders or falling too far back on their backside with their weight. However, if done correctly, it is great for keeping the head on the ball and the front side closed.

- *Reaction Drills*. It's nice to have drills that players can fall back on to break up the monotony of practicing their hitting sometimes. I like to use a two-ball toss drill where the tosser tosses two balls to the hitter releasing the balls from his hand with one ball on top of the other.

The tosser then prompts the hitter with "top" or "bottom" and the hitter is suppose to hit the one the tosser has instructed him to hit. After a good soft toss regimen has been set where the players have shown improvement in their swings, I like to incorporate this drill. In my opinion, it is a good reaction drill for the hitting reflexes. There's not much time for a hitter to make a decision at the plate, especially if the count is not in the hitters favor. If the hitter's objective is to get the bat on the ball some how to move a runner or simply make something happen, he may be forced to take a swing that involves him committing to hitting the pitch, but then having to react in a defensive manner as the ball moves or breaks late. This is a good drill to try for those types of situations.

- *Soft toss and Tee Work.* In developing a fundamentally sound hitter, it has been my theme to incorporate soft toss and tee work into practicing hitting. In taking soft toss or in hitting from a tee, the height of the ball at contact should never be higher than the hitter's belt or lower than the knee. Between these two points on the hitter is where the majority of the pitches to them will be delivered. As important as it is for the ball to be hit at a certain height, it is equally important for the ball to be met at a particular location on the plate. The focus for soft toss or tee work should be for the ball to be hit up the middle or the other way. With this focus in mind, it is important to go back and think about what I mentioned earlier about where you want to meet those pitches in relationship to the plate: up the middle- middle part of the plate on the front half; other way- outside corner of plate on the back half. Kids don't like to toss in these locations. They like to toss the ball letter high and out in front. In doing this they are only working on hitting the inside pitch and quite honestly a rare homerun pitch at that height. Good pitchers will throw hitters low forcing a hitter to go with a pitch. That is a hard thing for a hitter to do. Pitchers will pitch inside, don't get me wrong, as well as make mistakes in their locations. However, a player will have a lot easier time adjusting to a pitch inside if his focus is away, then he will if his focus is for something inside to pull but is then delivered away. Focusing away gives the hitter coverage of the entire plate, where focus on the inside pitch eliminates the outside half of the plate leaving the hitter vulnerable.

Location of the toss or ball on the tee is important as well as the tosser. I like to have my players toss at a 45-degree angle in front of the hitter, because it gives more of a perception of where the ball will be coming from (which is in front of the hitter). You may be saying to yourself, but the ball does not come to the hitter from that angle? I understand that, however, my point is that many times I'll see players tossing directly to the side of the hitter facing him. I feel it gives a truer perception for the hitter to see the ball from in front of him rather than the side. It also gives a good visual for the hitter to understand how his bat should extend through the zone. If a hitter is getting proper extension and the most power out of his swing, his arms and bat should form a "Y" where the bat is pointing directly at the tosser. If the tosser is at a 45-degree angle and the focus for the hitter's extension is to be pointing at the tosser, then it is just easier, in my opinion, for the hitter to have the proper visual in mind for what a good swing will look and feel like.

Even better than tossing from an angle, I like to have players go in the cage, sit on a bucket behind an L-screen, and from about 15 feet away from home plate throw to a hitter like they're throwing darts. From this distance it is easy to control where the ball is being thrown (especially the height since it's delivered lower), therefore the thrower should try to throw everything on the outside half of the plate. The hitter should have the same focus as when tossing and try to hit the ball back from where it came. After hitting like this for a while, the hitter gets accustomed to trying to hit the L-screen on a line. They get accustomed to hearing the little ping that the sound of impact makes. If they're really driving through the ball, and hitting the screen square, it will probably move a little bit, too. All are good focuses and objectives for the hitter to have as well as fun for the hitter to try and execute.

Finally, the most important thing to remember in all of this is the amount of reps a hitter should take during one set of tee work, soft toss, or cage work. A hitter should never take more than 8 swings in one set, I feel. Going beyond 8 leads to a hitter losing focus mentally as well as physically becoming tired. Those two combinations put together lead to bad habits, which is what you, as a coach, are trying to break.

- *Field BP.* Whether pitchers throw live, coaches throw live, or players from a bucket behind an L-screen throw live, in taking BP on the field, there must be a set script in place for the hitter to follow. In swinging the bat the hitter should still focus on hitting the ball up the middle or the other way. The hitter also should still only get as many as 8 pitches to swing with. However, as a coach, you may want to instruct your hitters to bunt the first two, with one being down the 1st base line and then one down the 3rd base line. Maybe the third pitch might be a squeeze bunt or a hit and run swing, leaving the hitter with the last 4-5 swings being normal cuts. There should be a reward system in place so that if a hitter is executing his bunts properly or his situational hitting properly, he can have additional swings added on to the 4-5 cuts already reserved. While the player at the plate is executing his bunts for a particular set, there can be two players "in the hole" waiting for their BP with fungoes or bats in hand hitting ground balls to infielders. As a hitter finishes his reps at the plate, he could run the bases by sprinting to 1st on his last swing. From first work on his lead and jump to 2nd as the next hitter sacrifices a bunt down the 1st base line. The same idea then from 2nd to 3rd as the hitter sacrifices the third base line. From third, the runner could simulate a squeeze play, if that is next for hitter in his reps, or run on contact, or tag on a fly...I think you get the idea. Everything should have a purpose.

***

Repetition, Repetition, Repetition. You have to stay on these kids. You have to repeat what you tell them over and over again (just in different or creative ways). When they start to struggle, then get back to fundamentals. You can set a program for the kids to follow, whether it is at practice or for pregame BP, but either way, whatever you choose to do, the coach has to overlook the production and encourage focus. Otherwise, kids fall back on bad habits. After all, they can't see themselves swing. They may be struggling with no idea why. Your eyes are the key to their solution.

Pitching

The pitcher *is* the best athlete on the team. Let's make certain we understand that first. It takes a tremendous amount of strength, coordination, and conditioning to be a pitcher, in addition to intelligence and imagination. Any player can say he knows how to pitch and that he has 5 or 12 pitches, but it takes a significant amount of dedication to the idea of *being* a pitcher to truly find success on the mound. This is particularly tough at the teenage level because there is so much physical and emotional growth taking place, something as coaches we tend to forget. Physically, we have to remember that our freshman will not be able to handle the same sort of approach as we take with our seniors. Emotionally, may be even more important. The maturity is seldom there in a teenage player, no matter what the level is. As a coach we have to be sympathetic to that. With all players, coaches need to be careful in their handling of them and be cognizant of each player's individual needs. With pitchers, it may be even more important. For the most part, the team's fate falls in the hands of it's pitcher. How he performs will ultimately dictate the team's success. There's a significant amount of pressure there for one person to handle. How his coach, his parents, and his teammates deal with that person can have an impact taken with him beyond the field and later in life. O.K., O.K., maybe I'm getting a little to dramatic here, but speaking as a former pitcher in high school and college, I remember how each time I took to the mound there was that life or death feeling. That may have just been my personality, but with the approach I took to pitching and the work I put in beyond the field of play, I would hope that any pitching prospect I have the opportunity to deal with would have that same sort of mind set. If they do, I feel it shows how much they care.

There are several things that go into pitching. There's mechanics, conditioning, approaches to hitters, infield defensive, etc. The following breaks down the various points I look for in developing a younger pitcher:

Basic Throwing

A player looking to maximize his promise as a pitcher must first be able to throw with proper fundamentals. Really, any defensive player should have these fundamentals. Pitchers especially, because it enforces mechanics that help a player decrease the likelihood they will experience arm pain during their progression as a ball player. Many players will deal with different "growing pains" as they continue in their physical growth. The more a coach can do to institute the proper mechanics of throwing, the healthier the player can be.

When a player is playing catch with another player, there are a couple of things to look for. First, there is the pivot. The player's back foot (i.e.- a right hander's back foot would be his right one) should square up to his intended target and, in squaring up, the foot must pivot.

Much like a pitcher places his foot in front of the rubber in delivering a pitch to the plate, a player's pivot in playing catch is the same idea. If a line was drawn to the intended target, the player would plant his foot so that it ran perpendicular to that line. The reason this is

57

important, is the player's top half will align so that the shoulders are on line with the intended target. The common fault that many players have is that their back foot and front foot are positioned when they throw so that the toes are pointing towards the target. This leaves the player's upper half open making it difficult for him to get as much velocity and accuracy on his throw as well as puts added stress on the arm. It's surprising how poor a high school player's footwork is when he first comes to the high school ranks. This is something that should be stressed the first time a kid plays catch.

Once the feet are planted, the player's upper half is in proper alignment to throw the baseball. During the process of the player pivoting to throw, the hands go through the process of breaking to "field goal" position. Notice in the picture, the glove hand is ready to lead the upper half and the ball is held so that the fingers are on the part of the ball closest to the player's head (the ball actually is pointed in the opposite direction of the target).

From here, the player rotates his top half so that his shoulders are perpendicular to the intended target line (to do this, I've always felt that pulling with the lead elbow will get me into this position). The player's hand gets in a position so that it is behind the ball and the ball is pointing to the target. The glove hand has lowered to the player's side below shoulder level and the throwing arm is cocked with the hand position behind the ball ready to release through the baseball. The player's weight is transferred towards the front side as the arm comes forward. Note in the picture, the back foot is pushing from its original pivot position as the upper half rotates. At this position, the player's back foot may also appear more on his toe than what is pictured above. Either position is preferable. The point is the player's bottom half is engaged in the throw.

Notice the height of the elbow at shoulder level. Players need to be careful to not drop the elbow forcing them to "sling" the ball when they throw (when a player slings a ball, the ball is harder to control because of it's tailing spin as well as harder on the player's elbow). Now, the player releases the ball to the target following through with his hand so it finishes in a position where the player could touch the opposite hip to his throwing arm and his back is bent forward. The back pivot foot, during the throw, pushes off and finishes slightly in front of the lead foot. As the player follows through, it's important that their arm continues through to the hip.

Often, a player will only finish with the arm straight out in front of them. If they finish in this position, they have achieved the goal of getting good extension and throwing with a *long* arm. However, stopping the arm abruptly in front of the body can be hard on the player's elbow and shoulder.

Through this entire process, the player's entire body has been engaged in the throw taking as much of the stress off of the player's shoulder and elbow as possible. Without proper throwing fundamentals, a player is at risk of primarily throwing with his arm, which can lead to most of the common shoulder and elbow pains associated with throwing a baseball.

Follow Through

As it is important to implement with any player proper throwing fundamentals, an additional point to mention with regards to the previous topic is the specifics of the follow through. Sometimes a team will include in their warm up routine a segment where each player plays catch with his partner from one knee. In performing this drill the player's takes a knee on his pivot leg and the lead leg is bent in front with the player's foot flat to the ground. This drill isolates what should occur with the upper half of the body when a throw is made. It's a good drill because it gives the player less to think about since the mechanics of the lower half are left out. The player goes through the same steps as he would if he were playing catch from a standing position (i.e.- breaking the hands to field goal position, rotating the upper half, *following through*). It's the last step that is so noteworthy in this drill, especially for a pitcher, because it gives the player the idea the proper feel for what it is like to follow through properly. As opposed to playing catch from a standing position and having the throwing hand finish around the opposite hip, a pitcher who will have used his legs to stride more towards his target, will be lower to the ground and will want his throwing hand to finish so that it has come over the lead bent leg. It emphasizes proper follow through with the throwing arm as well brings the back into the sequence. The back will need to bend more from this position to help the throwing hand follow through, similar to the pitching sequence which we will explore more in depth later.

Bullpen Work

First of all, let me clarify what I mean by bullpen work. Essentially, bullpen work is any work that a pitcher puts in that simulates throwing from a mound. If there is a mound to work from, fine. If not, flat ground is probably more beneficial. Throwing from the flat ground, I feel, forces the pitchers legs to drive hard to the target and maximizes the body's influence in the pitcher's delivery. One might wonder, though, about the pitcher having to adjust to throwing off of a mound if he is getting all of his practice in on flat ground. He might wonder if the pitcher will throw the ball too low because he is not working down the hill of a mound. I think that's a nice problem to have since a pitcher's focus should be on keeping the ball down in the first place. The simple thought that the pitcher needs to throw *through* the catcher's mitt should be enough to get the pitcher to bring the ball back up to the zone as well as possibly get some added velocity. It's easier to correct a pitcher who throws a ball too low, than it is to correct one who throws too high.

When a pitcher gets his work in the bullpen, in warming up, I feel there should be two approaches to keep in mind. If it's early in the season or it's raining and the team is stuck practicing inside, chances are the pitcher has little room to play catch past 60 feet. If the pitcher has not had much time to warm up, I would have the catcher start from a standing position and the pitcher start from the base of the mound and simply focus on throwing to the standing catcher's chest. The pitcher should have the same thought process as when he is playing catch before practice or a game. His footwork and upper body should all have the same consistent motion that a fundamentally sound ball player should possess. As a pitcher, the leg kick may be exaggerated a bit more than the typical game of catch, and it may also be good practice for the pitcher to focus less on stepping into his pivot to throw. Instead he may start where the back foot is already perpendicular to the target line and simply bring the lead leg up as if the pitcher is throwing from the stretch. For every two or three tosses the pitcher should take a step back and keep doing so until the pitcher is throwing from about 5-10 feet behind the pitcher's rubber. Loosening up from behind the rubber allows the pitcher to get longer with the extension of his throwing arm, which is an important aspect of pitching for both velocity and longevity.

The second approach to warming up before getting in bullpen work is using the same approach the player should use before entering a game in relief. Assuming the pitcher has had time to play catch and throw at a reasonable length (in warming up before practice it would be in the player's best interest to reach a point where they are throwing from 100-120 feet), the pitcher should start throwing from the base of the mound and with each throw work his way back a step closer to the top. When the pitcher reaches the top of the hill, he should take 3-5 more tosses to a standing catcher. The catcher can then squat and the pitcher can get into his workout. After about 10-15 actual pitches from the mound, the pitcher should have the feeling that he is ready to throw in a game. Each time a pitcher has the opportunity to warm up in this fashion, he should have himself timed to the point where he feels ready and try to improve on this time each time he practices this approach. The important part for the coach to assess during this process is just how ready the pitcher truly is to enter a ball game. The pitcher needs to focus on warming up quickly in case he would have to during an actual game. However, he should be careful not to rush through his mechanics. Rushing can lead to bad habits, and then any purpose in this exercise is lost.

In working in the bullpen, a pitcher needs to have an organized approach. In any bullpen session, a pitcher should work on his fastball (2 and/or 4 seam) and his change-up.

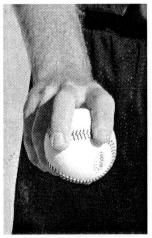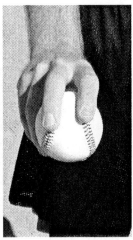

4-seam fastball is pictured above on the left side while the 2-seam fastball grip is pictured on the right.

He should focus on the points where he is spotting his pitches. Therefore, the catcher setting up on the corners, as opposed to the middle of the plate, is important. Breaking balls are important to add to the pitcher's arsenal of weapons to throw at a hitter, but mastering his location of the first two pitches is vital to the pitcher's success. It is also vital to strengthening the pitcher's arm.

Pitch count is important for the pitcher to understand in getting in his work. When practice is just beginning at the start of a new season, then a pitcher should probably limit himself to around 30 pitches. Each workout thereafter, the pitcher can increase that sequence by 5 additional pitches. I would wait with a pitcher to throw any breaking pitches until about the 3rd or 4th workout. In keeping in mind the amount of pitches and types of pitches to be thrown, the pitcher should work from the stretch as well as the wind up. If a player is new to the idea of pitching, it might be in that player's best interest to throw him from the stretch for the first few sessions. This cuts down on the thoughts of all of the mechanics of pitching and stresses more the balance and location involved in pitching.

With any pitching workout during practice, it is recommended that the pitcher does some running after the workout. The player should at least do enough running afterwards to the point where the heart rate has been accelerated and the player's developed a good sweat. This ensures the player has his blood flowing throughout his entire body and the circulation in his arm is back to normal. I like to call this "getting the junk out" of the player's arm so that he will be able to rebound easier the next day with his throwing. After a little run, it would also be encouraged to have the player stretch his shoulder, legs and back, even if he has already done the same stretches previously in practice. Other conditioning, like work with light dumbbells can be incorporated as well, but will be discussed in greater detail later.

Finally, the question of how often a player should throw off of a mound to get his arm or keep his arm in shape for the season. Some coaches feel pitchers should throw everyday. I agree with those coaches if they mean they should be involved in some sort of throwing everyday. By throwing, it could be bullpen work, long toss, and reps in the field for those position players who also pitch, etc. I don't think a pitcher should throw a *pitching workout* every practice. If a pitcher gets some sort of workout in that focuses on mechanics and throwing to a catcher every other practice, then a pitcher after 4 weeks of practice (at 5 days a week) should be ready to go. Watching the pitchers pitch count early on during games will still be important, but that should be monitored at any point in the season given the fact the coach is dealing with young arms.

Long Toss

On days when a pitcher is not getting in his work in the bullpen, I like the idea of the pitcher playing some long catch. How long the catch is, depends on what you have to work with. If it means keeping a couple of players after practice to throw the length of the gym when things are less crowded, then that will have to do. Ideally, though, a pitcher should try to play some long toss to at least 120 feet. Obviously, the player should only use a fastball grip or even more specific, a 4-seam grip like a player would use playing in the field. Their technique should be similar to that in basic throwing before practice, only the longer the throw becomes the more active the feet should be. More of a crow hop into a pivot should be used to take strain off of the throwing arm and as the distance between the players increase a bit more loft should be added to the arc of the throw. As loft is added, the intention is the player is throwing with a long arm. It is not the intention for the player to lob the ball to his partner. In playing catch at this distance, the idea of the player adding strength to his arm is the goal.

After no more than ten minutes of throwing at this distance, the player should decrease the distance a couple of steps for every throw so that he can gain control of the muscles in his arm again at a shorter distance. I like this approach in my pitcher's playing long toss as well as my player's simply warming up before practice for the same reasoning. The only difference is that I encourage my position players to work more on receiving the ball at their chest with two hands and getting into a quick release throwing position to get the ball back to their partner. This is all done to stay consistent with their motions in the field.

Conditioning

In considering a pitcher's conditioning, there are four ingredients worth considering. The first would be the work that takes place in the weight room. In dealing with teenagers, high school will be the first time many are introduced to the idea of working with weights. Therefore, setting a specific program for pitchers to follow is not as important as simply having a consistent workout that gets them ready to play baseball.

In high school, whether dealing with freshmen or seniors, it is equally important to approach weight lifting with sets performed with several reps. Less weight, lifted in an explosive, controlled manner is more important to a baseball player than lifting a significant amount of weight that can only be lifted at 3-5 reps to build mass. Baseball players should focus first on flexibility. Especially, if these players are younger and still growing. For players who are older and bigger, then approaching weight lifting with the idea of building mass can be incorporated more as long the other approach is still considered. No matter what weight exercise is performed, it is important for the player to lift the weights with proper technique. It also is important for the player to perform exercises that balance each other. By this, I am suggesting if a player works out his chest, then he also needs to work out his back. If he works out his biceps, then he should also work out his triceps, etc.

Although a pitcher can benefit from a solid weight regimen, at the very least, a pitcher, and really every player, should engage on a consistent basis in some sort of light dumbbell or rubber band routine. Performing these exercises (also known as jobe exercises) at 3 sets of 10 reps each 3-4 times a week can be a tremendous asset to the pitcher in maintaining a healthy arm. The following are all good exercises to perform to help the player build shoulder strength and flexibility. Note: even though the exercises are performed in the pictures using 5 pound dumbbells, similar exercises can be performed using rubber tubing:

Arm extensions

Supraspinatus

Rainbows (Great for the shoulders!)

Crossovers

Lat Flies

External Rotations

Internal Rotations

Front Rotator Cuff Stretch (Stretching all parts of the rotator cuff is important, however, stretching the front part of the muscle is vital because of the forward stress that is placed on the shoulder during the execution of the pitching motion)

Arm hangs (There are several exercises that can be done from this starting position. The player can swing the dumbbell right to left and front to back. In doing this, the dumbbell swings about a foot from it's original position to either side. The player can also swing the weight in a clockwise motion follow by a counter-clockwise rotation. All 4 of these exercises are a great way to get a good stretch on the shoulder)

In addition to dumbbell exercises, if no weight program is being performed on a regular basis, it would be in the player's best interest to include a regimen of push-ups, pull-ups, tricep dips and even some jump rope. Anything extra to add to a player's upper body strength would be beneficial.

Earlier, I stressed the importance of the pitcher including some sort of running with his pitching workout. Whether it is the off-season or in-season, a pitcher should be engaged in some sort of running routine. There are a couple of schools of thought that coaches debate on when it comes to handling their pitcher's running. One school of thought is the belief that when pitchers do any sort of running to condition, it should be done so in a sprinting manner. After all, baseball is a game built around having to do things in spurts (i.e.-sprint around the bases, sprint after the ball defensively, etc.). The other school of thought is that a pitcher should run long distances to build endurance so they can throw higher pitch amounts during a game and not *lose their legs*. Personally, I don't have a significant preference. I like to see my pitchers once or twice a week going for about a 2-3 mile jog. I also like to run my entire team through some sort of sprinting exercise at the ends of practices that involve base running as conditioning. Because I am dealing with players that are still going through growing spurts, I do have to be careful of the impact that their knees and other joints may take from running long distances on harder surfaces. Many players have never run long distances in their life before coming to our program so expecting them to run 2 or 3 miles, even at a jog, is not fair to ask. A good compromise to sprinting versus long distance running is to have players run stairs or hills. The player sprints up, jogs down, and in doing so, is building the muscles that will allow him to drive hard off the mound using his legs and endure over several innings.

The more running options used, the easier it is for the player to stay motivated to work to get better. The same old routine can get monotonous and varying it can keep things fresh. On pitching days, maybe the pitcher can run hills or stairs after his workout, where on long throwing days, he can do distances. Either way, try to vary it.

Finally, a pitcher should have a consistent set of abdominal exercises to perform. Stronger abs. means a stronger back, yet another integral part of a pitcher's effectiveness. I like to see my pitcher's involved in an ab. routine whether it is the off-season or as a part of their pitching workouts. Usually, our pitchers will throw in pairs for their bullpen workout. While one throws, the other does some dumbbell work and ab. exercises. When they're both finished on the mound, they do their running.

There are many different ab. exercises a player can engage in. Something, as simple as a basic crunch or traditional sit up would be a great place to start. Incorporating a medicine ball into the routine can also be beneficial. A couple of examples of ab. exercises that include the use of a medicine ball, which I would suggest:

- In performing a traditional sit up the player could begin with a medicine ball held above his head and as he begins his accent up, he throws it to his partner who is standing and holding the player's feet in place with his feet. As the player begins his decent back to the starting position, his partner delivers the ball back to the player's chest. At the bottom of the sit up, the player returns the medicine ball to the original starting position above his head to repeat the process.

- Another exercise that could include the traditional sit up and the inclusion of the medicine ball would involve the player holding the ball straight in front of him and rotating the ball left and right as he makes his accent (once to the left, once to the right). On the decent, the player repeats the rotation.

Note: With any abdominal routine, I would suggest performing the exercises in sets of 3 with each set consisting of 10 repetitions.

Mechanics

In helping a pitcher develop fundamentally sound mechanics there are several things to look for in their delivery. Similar to hitting, each pitcher is his own individual and may do many things well in his delivery to the plate or may have to make several adjustments to maximize his success on the mound. If there is one aspect that I notice in a pitcher's mechanics that could be improved, sometimes the best thing to do with that player is to put him into the position I'm trying to help him improve upon and make some tosses (at half speed) from there. If there are several things that a pitcher needs to work on in his delivery, then pick out one or two things to key in on per workout session and possibly deemphasize the importance of hitting particular spots with the catcher. If a pitcher is just beginning, start him from the stretch to simplify the motion. Starting from the stretch can eliminate the first few steps, thus eliminating excess thoughts. Either way, the following is what I look for in my pitchers:

1. **Set up on the mound:** I feel how the pitcher positions his feet on the rubber from the wind up position should be a matter of comfort. Traditionally, a right-hander will take his place with toes pointing towards the plate on the right side of the rubber and a lefty will set up on the left side. Why? Well, the reasoning is the angle at which the pitch will be delivered to the hitter allows the pitcher to hide the ball from the hitter a split second longer. Is this a big deal? I don't think so. As a left-handed pitcher, I felt more comfortable throwing from the right side of the rubber (probably because I grew up throwing out of the hole that right handers would leave behind). Since my mechanics were sound, my starting foot position from the rubber became an insignificant detail.

2. **Starting the windup:** To begin the pitchers
   motion to the plate, the pitcher takes a
   relatively small step back or slightly to the side.
   Notice I'm saying *or* here. The important part to
   look for is what is happening with the upper part
   of the pitchers body. If the upper half is still
   consistent with the pitcher's starting position, in
   other words, there is no significant lean to the
   side or back, then that would be ideal. If there
   is a lean with the upper half, that would be
   allowable. A *slight* lean forward would be o.k.

The first picture in this sequence illustrates a step to the side, while the second shows a step behind the rubber. The above pictures show a side view of the start of the windup. The purpose of these two illustrations is to show that the pitcher's weight in the upper half is not leaning too far back. The picture on the left shows an upper half in proper position, while the right illustration shows what to avoid.

The hands position, during this process, depends on where the pitcher starts with them. If the pitcher starts with his hands to his side, then the hands should come together during the step back and end up no higher than the pitcher's head and no lower than his chest. This idea of where the hands are after the step back would hold true also if the player started with his hands together at the belt, near the chest, or at head level. If a player prefers to take his hand above his head, that's acceptable as long as his upper half does not lean too far back. Excessive motions in the mechanics of pitching allow for more error to take place and more energy to be exerted. I like a pitcher to start with his hands together in front at about chest level so he can get a good grip on the pitch he is going to deliver. As the pitcher steps back, I prefer the pitcher to not raise his hands too much. Again, I'm speaking as a coach who has seen time on the mound. I felt this is something that worked best for me for the reasons I have stressed, but it may not be the way to go with all pitchers. The important aspect here is position of the upper half and controlling the direction its weight is being distributed.

3. **Pivot to Balance:** From the second position, the pitcher plants his drive leg foot (for a right hander this would be the right leg) parallel to and still touching the pitching rubber.

The lead leg is lifted (not swung around) leading with the knee to a position where the hands have returned to chest level, the knee is at belt level, the front foot is pointing downward, and the drive leg is slightly bent. At this position, if a pitcher is in control of his mechanics, he should be able to balance on his back leg.

This is one of the most important things to look for in a pitcher's delivery, I feel. The tendency for most pitchers is to lose their balance forward. In order for a pitcher to start his motion towards the plate, his hands should break first. The lead leg driving down the mound along the target line to the catcher lead by the foot and not the front knee swinging open follows this.

The drive leg is engaged and has bent a bit more to allow the pitcher to *drive*, or push, off the rubber. The front foot lands on the ball of the foot pointing towards the plate either on the target line or *slightly* to the left of the line (for a right handed pitcher). The arms and hands have arrived in the field goal position (at least with the throwing arm) in the same manner mentioned earlier when we looked at basic throwing.

If a player is not able to balance from the top of his motion and is falling towards the plate before his hands get a chance to break, more effort and strain is placed on the pitcher's shoulder to throw the ball to the plate. From an endurance standpoint, this hurts the pitcher. Even more importantly, from a health standpoint, this can injure a pitcher.

4. **Rotation to Follow Through:** Essentially, we have arrived to the part of the motion that takes us back to how we play catch. For a pitcher to maximize the velocity at which he is going to deliver the baseball to the plate, starting from a standing position, the previous

three points are important. However, now, the pitcher is basically in a position that is similar to throwing from his knee during pre practice warm up. The only difference is his back leg is not positioned so the knee is bent and touching the ground. It's instead at the point where it is ready to drive off of the rubber.

Simultaneously, the upper half rotates from field goal position to the point where the throwing arm is finishing across the lead leg's knee (just as it does during the knee drill) and the back leg is pushing off the top of the mound coming around to a point where it is practically even with or slightly past the lead foot.

The pitcher has used his lead elbow to rotate the upper half and is using his back to follow through to a position where he should be fairly bent over at his waist with both knees bent. Often, pitchers will finish stiff legged with their lead leg and/or not bend much at the waist. In doing this, they're forcing their upper body to do most of the work, which, again, is not maximizing their potential. Some player's may lack the flexibility to finish as I have in the pictures I've included (which honestly for a teenage kid is sad). Keeping after these players to put forth an effort to focus and take pride during stretching both before and after practice is essential to help them improve this problem.

5. **5th infielder:** Finally, the ball is on the way and the actual delivery part is complete. However, the pitcher's job has not finished. A good pitcher should have faith in his defense and, while strikeouts are nice, should try to make pitches that force the hitters to put the ball in play so the defense has a good opportunity to make the out for the pitcher. While there are four infielders whose sole purpose is to provide that defense for their pitcher, the pitcher himself can be just as important. A pitcher who has sound mechanics should finish in a position so that he is able to quickly recover to an infielder's set up.

A pitcher can help himself by snagging ground balls or line drives hit back up the middle (like a good hitter should try to do), or by running down a bunt to get a force at a base. Other benefits to finishing in a good defensive position, allow the pitcher to chase down foul balls or cover 1st base. The point is, the better the mechanics of the pitcher, the better the defense becomes.

Other Thoughts

- **Developing Pitches-** Every player during practice needs to approach each drill with a purpose or a goal. In pitching, players cannot afford to waste their efforts during their bullpen sessions and simply go through the motions to get work in. Pitchers need to try and take something from every session to help themselves continue to improve. It's harder with younger players, when they do play other positions and practice resources available and/or time are limited. Therefore, every second of practice a player has to work on some aspect of pitching is priceless. Starting with playing catch before practice begins, pitchers, as with everyone else, should work on getting loose. However, while they are doing this, they can work on their different grips with certain pitches. It's in every pitcher's best interest to develop at least a change up to compliment their fastball. They should play catch working on the 2 and 4 seam fast ball grips, as mentioned before, but also work on finding a comfortable change up grip. There are various grips to try, but it is a matter of personal preference which one will work best for a player. Off speed pitches are feel pitches and every pitcher will have their own idea of what is comfortable and what is not. Some of the more common change up grips I have picture below, but with any grip, it is worth noticing that there are more fingers on the ball and the ball is positioned deeper in the hand as opposed to the fastball which is towards the fingertips.

In throwing this pitch, everything is the same as the fastball motion all the way down to the grip pressure used to hold the ball. The speed of the pitcher's arm *does not slow down.* There is more covering the ball, therefore there is more for the ball to overcome to be released from the hand causing the ball to lose velocity. This is why it is important to keep a nice relaxed grip and try to throw the pitch as hard as the fastball. In addition to traditional change ups, if a pitcher has lanky or slim fingers, a split finger or forkball might be a good idea to experiment with.

The split finger grip (left) and forkball grip (right)

Again, the arm speed is the same as the fastball only in delivering the pitch, the pitcher drags his toe off of the rubber causing the arm to pull through harder and the ball to have more drop on it.

In addition to having a good change up, a high school ball player should develop a good breaking ball. I'm a big believer in not teaching a curveball to any player until they've at least reached the high school level. If a player can work on his fastball and change up first, he is building strength in his arm that, by the time he reaches high school, can help his arm handle the strain of throwing a breaking ball. Again, I have included some grips worth trying in throwing a curveball, but just like the change up, it is a feel pitch that a pitcher needs to experiment with until he finds something that is comfortable.

2 possible curveball grips

The arm speed in throwing a breaking ball remains the same just as it would look throwing a fastball or change up. The difference in delivering a curveball as opposed to the other two pitches, is at the top of the delivery where a fastball or change up grip has the hand positioned behind the ball, the hand is now positioned more to the side away from the pitcher's head. For the ball to break down and away from a right handed hitter, the fingers will be more to the side of the ball as opposed to a pitch that will break more top to bottom where the fingers are closer to the top of the ball.

This series of pictures shows the difference between the hands position on the baseball as the pitcher's arm arrives at the top of his delivery. The above picture illustrates the fastball position, while the picture on the proceeding page shows the curveball at the top

The key to developing a good curveball is maintaining consistent fastball arm speed and *pulling through* the pitch. A great drill to try to simulate that feel is to have a player throw an empty tennis can starting with his hand positioned at the top of the can. The way the can rotates through the air gives the pitcher immediate feedback as to whether he is getting the rotation he wants. It also forces the player to reach out in front and release the ball in front of his head as opposed to behind where the pitch would tend to "hang" in the strike zone. By releasing the ball in front the pitch comes off with a flatter appearance to the hitter making it harder to pick up the break.

- **Developing Command of Pitches-** During every bullpen session it's been discussed how important it is for the pitcher to work on hitting "spots". The pitcher needs to be able to hit the catcher's mitt on either corner with his fastball or change up and not expose himself to leaving the pitch over the middle of the plate. He also needs to work on throwing his breaking ball for strikes as well as for "waste" pitches. As a pitcher, can the player throw a curveball for a strike when down in the count 3-1 or 2-0? As a coach, I know I want to have enough confidence in my pitchers to execute a strike with a curveball or change up so that I can call that pitch in a given situation. Does he know where to throw a breaking ball, and even a fastball, when he's ahead in the count 0-2 or 1-2? Curveballs should have the appearance that they are a fastball, but it finishes by breaking down and out of the strike zone. Fastballs can be wasted higher in the zone simulating the start of a breaking ball that never breaks. These are all things that need to be addressed and mastered during bullpen sessions. Better yet, they should be mastered during game simulated situations if possible during practice.

- **Working from the Stretch-** During any bullpen session, it is important for a pitcher to throw somewhere between 25 to 35% of his pitches from the stretch. I feel that many sessions in the bullpen should start from the stretch Starting from the stretch forces the player to start by pitching within himself. He's not winding up so his weight should not fall forward when he gets to his balance point as discussed in the mechanics section. The pitcher simply lifts his leg straight up to the balance position and, with everything in position, is ready to drive to the plate.

While throwing from the stretch the pitcher needs to simulate the idea that there are runners on to hold. Stepping off every once in a while and simply working on his footwork to pick off a runner from first or second is good to work on for a couple of reasons. One, it gets the pitcher comfortable with the proper technique to use to throw to the bases.

Second, it forces him out of a predictable rhythm, which is a common problem for many young pitchers. A pitcher should be aware of how much time he is taking to deliver the ball to the plate after coming set. He should try to vary these times just as he should in a game to keep the runner from getting too comfortable with his lead and jumps from the bases.

Proper step off

Two illustrations of the right-hander's pickoff move to first. The picture on the left shows the pitcher's footwork after stepping off first, while the picture on the right demonstrates a 90-

degree rotation of the feet from the pitchers stretch position on the mound.

Finally, in working from the stretch, it is worth discussing the slide step. I would rather see a pitcher work on having solid mechanics and on varying his time to the plate first, before throwing in a slide step. I also would like to see the slide step only used by players as they get older and, more importantly, stronger. To execute the slide step the stretch set up remains similar. The pitcher may widen his feet just a bit in his set up and physically try to create the feeling that he is "packing the hip" with his drive leg. By this, I mean he is creating a sensation where he can *explode* off the mound with his back leg.

In delivering to the plate, the pitcher breaks his hands and simultaneously the pitcher drives to the plate with his front foot lifting far enough off the ground to clear the dirt and plant down the target line. Breaking the hands as soon as the motion starts gives the pitcher the best chance to prevent dragging his arm and helps keep the velocity up on the pitch. It's a tough move to master, which requires a lot of coordination and natural ability on the pitcher's part. As a coach, I would rather see the pitcher try to cut down on any excess movements in their motion (like his leg kick) off the stretch and work on holding the runner on.

***

I haven't discussed much about dealing with arm pain or icing down shoulders after throwing off the mound. I only have my own experiences with arm pain and physical therapy to go off of in addressing these topics. However, it is my feeling that there is good arm pain and there is bad arm pain. Good arm pain involves the pitcher's muscle in his arm and is usually a result of fatigue. Bad arm pain usually involves the tendons or ligaments and could be various things. Having a good trainer handy is an asset. The more I coach, the more I learn. My advice is if you don't know what to tell a player, tell him to see the trainer or his doctor. Don't suggest ice when heat might be the best route and vice versa. As far as icing the arm after throwing, I have never felt it is a big deal. As a player, I seldom did it. I thought if I could do a little running after throwing, then the blood would get back to circulating in a normal fashion in the arm aiding in its recovery time. Icing after running and throwing, in my opinion, isn't going to hurt. Icing after just throwing, I don't feel helps the recovery process.

Coaches have to use common sense, too. Most of the player's we deal with at the teenage level are not solely going to be pitchers. After all, sticking with the thought that pitcher's are the best athletes on the team, they're going to be shortstops, outfielders, etc. They'll most likely play a position that is demanding on the arm in the amount of reps it takes to be successful at that position.

Pitcher's should have the most structured routine on the team. However, if a pitcher is an outfielder or shortstop that has to make several throws from a longer distance, then long toss for him in his pitching workout is probably less important. On days after these player's pitch, maybe instead of playing them in the field the next day DH them, or, if you can get away with it, rest him. Our seasons are long and our arms are young. The coach needs to be careful and knowledgeable in how he deals with his pitching staff.

About the Author

Jeff Gutjahr is getting set to start his 6th season as a baseball coach at Kirkwood High School in St. Louis, Missouri. Before coming to Kirkwood, Jeff completed his degrees in Education and Mathematics at Webster University also in St. Louis. While at Webster, he played for the school's baseball team enjoying all-conference honors all 3 of his seasons as an outfielder and pitcher. His book, A Coach's Handbook, is a collection of thoughts on hitting and pitching meant to help those who teach the game communicate more effectively to their players.

Printed in the United States
23757LVS00001B/312

9 781414 027784